Miracles Never Cease!

Oral Roberts
William DeArteaga
Paul Thigpen
Jack Deere

TOOLS FOR SPIRIT-LED LIVING
ORLANDO, FLORIDA

Printed in the United States of America
Library of Congress Catalog Card Number: 92-75729
International Standard Book Number: 0-88419-332-2

Creation House
Strang Communications Company
190 North Westmonte Drive
Altamonte Springs, FL 32714
(407) 862-7565

CONTENTS

INTRODUCTION

This is not a book about formulas or how to get God to answer your every prayer instantly with an astounding miracle. It is about the fact that countless miracles have occurred throughout the history of the church and are continuing even today.

This is especially true in the Third World where their skepticism is not so well developed. Miracles and supernatural gifts are a regular part of the work of missionaries — even those sent out by denominations that would not think of allowing such things in their North American churches.

Jesus could do no miracles in His hometown because of the people's unbelief (see Matt. 13:58).

Much of the church in America has adopted a world view which has what some have called an *excluded middle*. God operates way up high in heaven, and we operate way down here on the earth. The middle part of that world view — in which the two worlds touch by means of miracles, angels and visions — is excluded.

Consequently, unbelief is a fundamental part of the way many of us Western Christians think. Though we still hang on doctrinally to the supernatural, we really do not expect it to be part of our everyday lives. As Christians we should live in the anticipation of the miraculous.

Some people say miracles do not happen anymore because they have never seen one. Perhaps after having prayed sincerely on one occasion, a need was not met or no healing took place. As a result they concluded that, like a housekeeper who doesn't do windows, God doesn't do miracles.

Disappointment and grief are powerful forces that can be devastating to faith. They can lead you to view every promise of God in the light of your greatest disappointment. Those who follow such a course can be in danger of becoming, as the apostle Paul said, shipwrecked with regard to their faith.

Those who have seen no miracles can only say this: They have seen no miracles — at least nothing they recognized as a miracle. That does not mean miracles do not happen — only that they have never observed one.

Belief in the miraculous sometimes makes people very uncomfortable. Each difficulty can become a personal challenge to what they believe about God and His Word. After all, when you believe in miracles, every problem that comes your way is a test of faith.

It is always easier to be in a passive role than to wrestle with God and with your faith. It is also easier to plan each minute of a worship service than it is to wait on God to move supernaturally in a public meeting. A well-known Christian leader once commented that if the Holy Spirit were taken out of the world, most church services would go on as scheduled.

It is human nature to design our services and our beliefs in such a way that nothing is at risk. If God does not come through, nothing will be upset. The problem is, however, religion that can even work without God will eventually become an empty shell — the form of religion without the power.

Others reject the supernatural on the basis that the death of the twelve apostles marked the end of all miracles — despite testimony to the contrary from Christian leaders of every century (see chapter 2, "Did the Power of the Spirit Ever Leave the Church?"). The assumption is that God divided time into seven different dispensations and that no miracles can occur in the dispensation in which we now live — the church age.

Neither the Gospels nor the New Testament writers ever described such a system. Unfortunately, these doctrinal assumptions have become so fixed in people's minds that they are assumed to be infallible and are used to interpret the meaning of Scripture itself. This approach — of assuming that theological traditions are infallible — was precisely how the Pharisees of Jesus' day misunderstood the Law of Moses.

Still others reject miracles on philosophical and

scientific grounds. They assume miracles *do* not happen because they *can*not happen. These are the modern-day equivalents of the Sadducees, the Jewish religious leaders who did not believe in angels, miracles or resurrection. It is a short leap from believing God does not do miracles anymore to believing they never happened.

Actually, there is no good reason to believe an Almighty God either cannot or will not intervene in the natural course of things — especially when He keeps on doing it. Perhaps you have experienced God's miracle-working power firsthand. If so, drop me a note. I would love to hear about your miracle.

Walter L. Walker
Editorial Director
Creation House

ONE

QUENCHING THE SPIRIT

Today, as in Jesus' day, the Holy Spirit is often opposed by religious defenders of the status quo.

BY WILLIAM DEARTEAGA

At the heart of the Gospel accounts lies a startling irony. When Jesus came to reconcile the world to God, He reached out to unorthodox Samaritans, dishonest tax collectors and despised harlots. But He denounced with terrifying indignation the one group of people in His society who claimed to know better than anyone else how to please God: the Pharisees.

"You snakes!" Jesus dared to call them. "You brood of vipers! How will you escape being condemned to hell?" (Matt. 23:33). They were the most religious of people, yet Jesus saw that their arrogance and hypocrisy had ultimately led them astray from the God they claimed to serve.

Sadly enough, the Pharisees are with us yet. Though a number of disturbing characteristics identify the modern pharisaical party, we might say simply that a Pharisee is a deeply religious person who staunchly asserts and defends the status quo with regard to tradition, order and doctrine. Pharisees typically contend for what could be called *consensus orthodoxy* — that is, the theological interpretations accepted by most religious people of the day.

Most often Pharisees practice religion conscientiously to the point of legalism. But this is not the most serious error in their spirituality. Worse yet is the tendency of Pharisees to exaggerate the traditions and truths of consensus orthodoxy in order to oppose any new work of the Holy Spirit. Ultimately, then, the Pharisees' greatest offense is this: They oppose the work of God from *within* the church.

Pharisaism as a Heresy

Because Pharisees fight to defend the doctrinal status quo, they often spend their time as heresy hunters, pointing their fingers at one group after another with accusations of unorthodox teaching. Ironically, Pharisaism itself fits the biblical definition of heresy.

In the New Testament the Greek word translated as "heresy" is *hairesis*, which simply denotes a sect, faction or party. The Pharisees are described as an *hairesis* twice in the book of Acts (see Acts 15:5 and 26:5, where the word has been translated as "sect" or "party").

From the references to *hairesis* in the epistles,

we can conclude that certain sects have beliefs and practices that are deeply destructive and not just theologically mistaken. In 2 Peter 2:1 these groups are called "destructive heresies" because they take people out of spiritual fellowship with the body of Christ.

The New Testament points to two sects that were indeed spiritually deadly. These groups represent two types of heresy that have remained in one form or another throughout the history of the church. One was the Gnostic sects that plagued the congregations founded by Paul. The other was Pharisaism.

The Gnostics believed, among other things, that the material world was evil and in opposition to the spiritual world, which was good. As a result, the Gnostic way of spirituality accepts visions, prophecies and spiritual experiences without any restraint. In effect, Gnostics — both ancient and modern — do not discern between the activities of lower, demonic spirits and the inspiration of the Holy Spirit.

Pharisaism, on the other hand, takes exactly the opposite approach to dealing with spiritual experiences. Unlike the Gnostics, the Pharisees restrict the flow of spiritual experiences until religion becomes a purely intellectual and theological exercise. As a result, the Spirit is quenched.

Pharisaism in Scriptural Context

All the characteristics we typically associate with the Pharisees — hypocrisy, legalism, the reduction of scriptural interpretation to nit-picking — were exposed by Jesus' sharp words as He preached to the crowds at the temple (see Matt. 23). But these characteristics, which were actually the end product of a long spiritual process, were just symptoms of the problem.

Contrary to our common understanding of heresy, Pharisaism was a destructive heresy in spite of its theological correctness. Jesus made this point when He told the people: "The Pharisees sit in Moses' seat. So you must obey them and do everything they tell you. But do not do what they do, for they do not practice what they preach" (Matt. 23:2-3).

The Pharisees, Jesus said, were the inheritors of Moses' learning, the official expositors of the law. Jesus accepted the general correctness of their teaching — so it wasn't the Pharisees' specific theology but their *way of life* that placed them in opposition to the kingdom of God.

The Pharisees' real problem came from two sources. First, they drastically overvalued the role of theology in spiritual life and made theological correctness the chief religious virtue. Somewhere in the process, the primary command to love God and humankind was subordinated to correct theology.

Second, they had a mistaken confidence in their theological traditions as the perfect interpretation of Scripture. They falsely placed their group's theology — referred to in the Gospels as "the traditions of the elders" — on the same level as Scripture. It would be fair to say that this was the main issue of contention between Jesus and the Pharisees.

For example, the Pharisees were grievously offended by Jesus and His disciples for not ceremonially washing before eating (Matt. 15:2-6). Washing before meals was not part of the Mosaic law, but they had become so attached to their tradition that they were scandalized. They mistook their traditions about Scripture — their instrument for interpreting and applying God's Word — for Scripture itself.

Jesus kept the Law of Moses recorded in Scripture perfectly. Yet it seems He made a point of violating the traditions of the elders on a regular basis.

Jesus came to bring new understanding to what the Word of God really meant; but because the Pharisees were stuck in their consensus orthodoxy, they wound up opposing the move of the Spirit.

Judging by Origins

Because of their obsession with tradition and "correct" theology, the Pharisees' faith became highly intellectual. Faith, defined by the Old Testament patriarchs as *trust* in God and *expectancy* with regard to His provision, began to be understood as adherence to specific theological and ritual positions. The center of faith moved from the heart to the head. A sign of this was the way in which the Pharisees bombarded Jesus with theological questions.

As a natural result of their intellectualism, the Pharisees split into factions among themselves. We should note that divisions occur whenever the intellect is enthroned as the measure of spirituality — not because spiritual gifts are exercised, as many charge.

Pride of scholarship and intellect led the Pharisees to assume that all spiritual issues should be evaluated by solely theological means. True discernment, however, is an activity of the Holy Spirit within the person, in conjunction with intellectual and theological concepts.

The Pharisees evaluated religious questions and spiritual phenomena on the basis of authoritative traditional opinion rather than spiritual discernment. The principal criteria of judgment for them became the *origin* and *pedigree* of the person or opinion: Did the person manifesting spiritual power, such as healing or exorcism, have the right to that power by nature of training and association with the proper rabbinic school?

In Jesus' cleansing of the temple, for example, the principal concern was Jesus' *authority* for the act, not the justice of the act itself. The temple did need cleansing of its hucksters, but in the eyes of the religious leaders Jesus didn't have the rabbinical credentials for the task (see Mark 11:27-33).

Eventually their suspicion of spiritual phenomena became so intense that the Pharisees assumed that *all* spiritual phenomena of unknown "pedigree" were dangerous. That was why they disdained Peter and John's healing of a lame man — the two apostles were "uneducated, common men" who did not belong to a rabbinical school (Acts 4:13, RSV).

Flawed Discernment

Jesus completely short-circuited the Pharisees' system of rabbinical authority, proper origins and pedigrees when He declared that spiritual questions must be evaluated by their *fruit* (see Matt.

7:15-18). "Beware of the false prophets," He warned, "who come to you in sheep's clothing, but inwardly are ravenous wolves. You will know them by their fruits. Grapes are not gathered from thorn bushes, nor figs from thistles, are they?" (Matt. 7:15-16, NAS).

By His rejection of merely human traditions, Jesus did not mean that Scripture should be ignored. Rather He was pointing out the errors that people make when interpreting God's message. Such interpretations were human-made and subject to adjustment. So He affirmed that discernment is by fruit, not tradition — both in spiritual experiences and for conduct in areas of life where Scripture is not specific.

The contrast between the Christian view of spiritual accountability and discernment on the one hand (fruit) and the Pharisees' view on the other (origins) is summarized dramatically in the case of the man healed by blindness from birth (see John 9). When the Pharisees questioned the man and then his parents, they were not concerned with the fruit of the incident (that is, that the man had his sight restored) but rather with the origins and pedigree of the healer. They wanted to know what rabbinical school Jesus came from that authorized Him to do spiritual works. The Pharisees declared: "We are disciples of Moses! We know that God spoke to Moses, but as for this fellow [Jesus], we don't even know where he comes from" (John 9:28-29).

Jesus' injunction to judge the fruit of spiritual phenomena was extended by the Holy Spirit in Paul's epistles. He told the Thessalonians: "Do not quench the Spirit, do not despise prophesying, but test everything; hold fast what is good, abstain from every form of evil" (1 Thess. 5:19-22, RSV). Thus Paul, like Jesus, instructed his readers to test new things by attending to their fruits. And he specified in another epistle what exactly was good fruit: "love, joy, peace, patience, kindness, goodness, faithfulness, gentleness and self-control. Against such things there is no law" (Gal. 5:22-23).

This kind of testing has often been practiced in church history. The Holy Spirit knew that in the course of two thousand years or more the church would develop procedures not directly mentioned in the Bible, but still of God. For example, in the eighteenth century the institution of Sunday school was invented. After much discussion and testing of its fruit, the church found it excellent and adopted it.

Nevertheless, the fruit criterion should never be used to "test" those things plainly contrary to Scripture. For example, a person cannot "test" adultery followed by divorce, concluding that it wasn't sin because it produced the good fruit of a new, happier family. That is delusion. The original adultery was sin regardless of the subsequent feelings or even of the new children produced.

Distorted Faith

Jesus' ministry attacked and challenged not only the Pharisees' approach to discernment, but also their distorted definition of faith. In word and deed He reminded all who would listen that the primary meaning of faith was a trust-expectancy relationship with God. God would provide for the needs of the believer, deliver the afflicted from the kingdom of Satan, and do great and mighty works of power. Jesus understood that faith came from a direct relationship with God rather than the theology and rituals learned in rabbinical schools.

This did not mean that Jesus disdained theological knowledge and doctrine. Rather, in the total faith equation that He taught His disciples, faith-expectancy and trust in God were critically important, while theological expertise was of secondary importance.

Scripture clearly demonstrates the importance of faith over doctrine in two incidents: the exorcism of the daughter of the Canaanite woman (Matt. 15:21-28) and the healing of the centurion's servant (Matt. 8:5-13). In both cases the seekers had incorrect theology, according to religious leaders. Yet, despite their pagan beliefs, both had tremendous faith-expectancy that God used to grant their requests for healing through Jesus.

We cannot conclude that Jesus was affirming by silence the pagan doctrines of either seeker. Rather He praised and affirmed their faith-expectancy as a spiritual virtue and example for others. The right theology would come later through their relationship with Him.

A Hellish Spiritual Inheritance

Ironically, the Pharisees were once on the cutting edge of Judaism in opposing apostasy and paganism under the reign of a pagan Greek government. So in Jesus' day they assumed that their theological traditions — which had served well in the past — placed them in spiritual descent from the great prophets of the past. They expected

Judaism to develop and flower along lines they had charted. The Messiah would thus be a super-Pharisee who would resolve all their disputes by brilliant interpretations.

But Jesus' judgment of the Pharisees was considerably different from their self-evaluation: "You build the tombs of the prophets and adorn the monuments of the righteous, and say, 'If we had been living in the days of our fathers, we would not have been partners with them in shedding the blood of the prophets.' Consequently you bear witness against yourselves, that you are sons of those who murdered the prophets. Fill up then the measure of the guilt of your fathers" (Matt. 23:29-32, NAS).

Jesus' words are sobering. His assessment of the Pharisees: Because they opposed the Holy Spirit in His own generation (that is, in the person of Himself and His teachings), they had allied themselves with those who had opposed the prophets (and the Holy Spirit in the prophets) in former generations.

The principle still holds today. Present attitudes opposing the work of the Holy Spirit place a person in the hellish spiritual inheritance of the prophet-murderers. So believers must be willing and able to discern the work of the Holy Spirit for contemporary times.

We can begin to realize just how dangerous that spiritual inheritance is when we note that the Pharisees responded to Jesus' ministry and warnings of their dead spiritual state by accusing him of sorcery. The accusation had a certain logic to it, given their assumptions. Jesus worked miracles, yet neither He nor His disciples came from the established rabbinical schools. So His power, they concluded, had to come from illegitimate sources (see Matt. 12:24).

In His response to their accusations, Jesus described the unforgivable sin against the Holy Spirit: "Whoever shall speak a word against the Son of Man, it shall be forgiven him; but whoever shall speak against the Holy Spirit, it shall not be forgiven him, either in this age, or in the age to come" (Matt. 12:32, NAS).

We cannot ignore a critical issue here. Certainly witchcraft and sorcery are serious sins that require repentance to receive forgiveness. Yet to call something sorcery when it is in fact from God is more than a serious sin. Claiming that the works of the Holy Spirit are really the product of demonic activity "shall not be forgiven."

Regardless of how we interpret this text, this frightening statement alone should make Christians reluctant to accuse someone of sorcery for involvement in an unusual spiritual phenomenon. Such an accusation should come only after much study and prayer for discernment. Judgment of any healing or exorcism as demonic especially warrants caution.

Tragically, the Pharisees, in conjunction with the chief priests and Sadducees, at last conspired to eliminate the "sorcerer" Jesus by bringing false witnesses against Him. In view of the dangers of the moment, they thought that any means to stop Him, including a direct sin against the eighth commandment given to Moses, would be both politically expedient and spiritually acceptable (see Mark 14:56).

Thus Pharisaism, which had spent its energies in seeking elaborate ways to honor all the commandments, wound up breaking them in the crudest of ways.

Identifying the Pharisaical Spirit

Pharisaism continued to be a problem in the Jewish-Christian church of Jerusalem. For example, those Christians who had been Pharisees objected to Paul's practice of excusing gentile converts from circumcision and freeing them from the ritual laws of Judaism (Acts 15:5).

Through the succeeding generations even down to the present, the Pharisees have appeared again and again to divide and confuse the church.

So how can we avoid the pitfalls of pharisaical attitudes today? I would suggest several ways to identify Pharisaism and to separate it from the true Christian mandate to reprove error and not to be subject to every new wind of doctrine (see Eph. 4:14).

- People influenced by a spirit of Pharisaism will center their reproofs on the doctrinal status quo — the theological interpretations accepted by most religious people of the day.
- Modern-day Pharisees will seldom check the biblical evidence to see whether the issue under discussion exposes a weak point of their own theological tradition.
- Pharisaism is reluctant to wrestle responsibly with the fruit criterion. A revival will usually have "mixed fruit" insofar as the edges of the movement produce extremism and confusion. Yet a movement must be judged by its overall effect. Rather than discerning good and bad fruit within a movement, Pharisees make up their minds about it and then

seek evidence from the extremes to prove their points.

• Authentic Christian reproof has a quality of sadness and mercy, while Pharisaism is filled with righteous glee and a spirit of "I told you so!" Godly reproof hopes for repentance, correction and restoration. It also gladly recognizes the positive elements of those movements or people criticized. Pharisees do none of these things, and their only interests are in pointing out the errors and winning the cases.

A Contemporary Warning

The lesson to be learned from the Pharisees is clear. We must not grow so confident of our own human traditions, or so proud of our spiritual lineage, that we are blinded to the work of the Holy Spirit when it appears. Otherwise we might be found opposing God Himself and calling demonic what He has accomplished.

The immediate task of the church is to pray that the harm from the latest wave of Pharisaism will be dissipated quickly. With God's providential intervention, the confusion, division, fear and paranoia that have been loosed by the current Pharisees and witch-hunters could be turned to good. If the church can collectively learn that Pharisaism is indeed a perennial heresy and recognize it as it manifests, then the current crisis will have served as a painful but necessary landmark along the road to a higher level of discernment and spiritual maturity.

William DeArteaga is the author of *Quenching the Spirit*, a highly researched look at people and philosophies that have opposed the moves of the Spirit from the first century to today. He holds a master's degree in history from the University of Florida. DeArteaga and his wife, Carolyn, live in the Atlanta area, where he leads prayer and praise at his church.

This excerpt from DeArteaga's book, *Quenching the Spirit*, appeared in the September 1992 issue of *Charisma & Christian Life* magazine.

Quenching the Spirit (hardcover, 300 pages) may be ordered by sending $14.99 plus $2.50 for shipping and handling to Creation House, 190 North Westmonte Drive, Altamonte Springs, FL 32714. (Florida residents, please add $1.05 for sales tax.) The book should also be available at your local Christian bookstore.

TWO

DID THE POWER OF THE SPIRIT EVER LEAVE THE CHURCH?

The supernatural gifts of the Holy Spirit have always been with us, as a brief survey of church history demonstrates.

BY PAUL THIGPEN

Near the close of the fourth century, Augustine of Hippo — the brilliant Christian teacher whose writings have shaped Western thought ever since — pondered the lack of miracles in the Christian community of his day. His conclusion, stated simply in the tract *On True Religion*, seemed reasonable: Once the church had been established and extended throughout the world, "miracles were not allowed to continue" because they were no longer needed to "kindle" faith.

Yet nearly three decades later, in the final years of his life, Augustine found that things were not as they had seemed. Within the space of two years, believers in his North African diocese experienced a sudden wave of miraculous healings, seventy altogether. Unable to deny any longer that God was performing miracles, the aged bishop received the startling events with joy. He examined, verified and recorded each instance, asking for a written report from each person healed so he could publish the results and store them in his library as a compelling testimony to the pagan community.

Augustine's story illustrates the oft-repeated observation that people are more likely to be accurate about the things they affirm than the things they deny. Why is that? Because we tend to affirm the things we've experienced ourselves, matters in which we know what we're talking about. But we also tend to deny the things we haven't experienced ourselves — and that lack of experience, though we think it qualifies us to make generalizations, really only reflects ignorance.

In short, we tend to measure life's possibilities by our own limited experience. And as it was with Augustine, the temptation to deny the existence of things outside our own experience is nowhere more obvious than in the matter of spiritual gifts and the miracles they accomplish.

Some thirty years ago when the Pentecostal reality spilled over into the historic churches, creating the charismatic movement, testimonies about God's supernatural intervention in the modern world were met with deep skepticism. But, as the years passed and the evidence accumulated, many charismatic distinctives were accepted — and even adopted — throughout large portions of the church. Even many believers who still reject the practice of speaking in tongues have come to admit that healing, prophecy, exorcism, miracles and other spiritual gifts are still valid today.

In recent days, however, a second anti-charismatic "backlash" has been growing in some evangelical circles, particularly among fundamentalists. Their claim is basically the same one made a generation ago when the charismatic movement first made headlines: The miraculous gifts of the Holy Spirit, they claim, ceased soon after the first apostles passed away, so any movement that exercises such gifts cannot be of God.

Obviously, to evaluate the reasonableness of this position we must examine the annals of church history. Do the records show that the gifts of the Spirit ceased in the church after the first century? On the contrary. Even a brief sampling of historical documents from the last nineteen hundred years will show that the gifts — and the miracles they engendered — have never left the church.

The Early Centuries

The book of Acts depicts events in the infant church up to the middle of the first century A.D. But what happened next? In addition to the later New Testament books, a few ancient texts have survived to the present to shed some light on the beliefs and practices of the first-century Christian community.

One such book is the *Didache*, a manual on church discipline generally conceded to date from the latter part of the first century. In this work the author gives local congregations instructions for dealing with traveling prophets. Evidently, then, Christians at this point were still practicing the prophetic gifts of the Spirit.

This observation is confirmed by the writings of several bishops of the period who were known for their prophetic gifts, including Ignatius, the third bishop of Antioch, who followed the apostle Peter's successor in that office. Ignatius was born about the time of Jesus' resurrection and lived into the first decade of the second century.

In a letter to the church at Philadelphia, this highly respected church leader recalled how he had exercised the gift of prophecy to settle a dispute in the congregation. Though he could have appealed to his authority as a bishop, instead he cited the authority of the prophetic word. His comments show not only the continued operation of prophetic ministry, but also the high regard that prophecy still retained at the beginning of the second century.

Justin Martyr (c. 100-165), an early defender of the faith, noted in about 135 A.D. that Christian believers of his day possessed "gifts of the Spirit of God": "For one receives the spirit of understanding, another of counsel, another of strength, another of healing, another of foreknowledge, another of teaching, another of the fear of God." He made the point in an argument with the Jewish community in which he claimed that the charismatic gifts no longer appeared in Judaism because they had permanently passed to the church instead.

In a tract written to the Roman Senate, Justin made note of the supernatural ministry of Christians of that day: "Numberless demoniacs, throughout the whole world and in your city, many of our Christian men...have healed, and do heal, rendering helpless and driving the possessing devils out of the men."

The Shepherd of Hermas, written in the middle of the second century, described how prophets in the church of that day were filled with the Holy Spirit and then spoke forth the words of God. This particular book, itself an extended prophecy, was so highly respected by the early Christians that many considered it Scripture.

The life of Irenaeus (c. 130-200), bishop of Lyons in what is now France, takes us to western reaches of the Roman empire and the dawn of the third century. This famous opponent of early heresies threatening the church was explicit in his approval of valid prophetic ministry, going so far as to rebuke those who used the existence of false prophets as a pretext for "expelling the grace of prophecy" from the church.

Irenaeus spoke explicitly about the reality of charismatic gifts in the church of his day: "We have heard of many of the brethren who have foreknowledge of the future, visions and prophetic utterances; others, by laying on of hands, heal the sick and restore them to health.... We hear of many members of the church who have prophetic gifts, and by the Spirit speak with all kinds of tongues, and bring men's secret thoughts to light for their own good, and expound the mysteries of God."

Irenaeus also spoke of people raised from the dead. Some of the practices he described he had seen firsthand; others he heard about from reliable witnesses. In any case, he insisted, these gifts were not restricted to a local congregation but were present throughout the universal church.

A document recording the martyrdom of two Christian women in about 202 A.D., *The Passion of the Holy Martyrs Perpetua and Felicitas*, described prophetic revelations they received. The introduction of this work cites the words from the prophet Joel quoted by Peter on the day of Pentecost, noting that the words about prophecies, visions and dreams also apply to later generations. It goes on to say that the revelations to the martyrs were recorded "so that no weakness or despondency of faith may suppose that the divine grace abode only among the ancients."

During this same period Tertullian (c. 160-225), the greatest theologian of his day, was writing about the charismatic gifts. Though in his later years he joined a splinter group that became unbalanced in its prophetic ministry (the Montanists), Tertullian — while still with the orthodox church — instructed new Christians to come up out of the waters of baptism, praying and expecting the gifts of the Spirit to come upon them.

Eusebius (c. 260-340), the "father of church history," seemed to have taken a special interest in supernatural giftings. He spoke of how the church enjoys the gifts of the Holy Spirit, including the words of wisdom and knowledge, faith, healings and tongues. In addition, his histories contain numerous accounts of miracles and spiritual giftings in operation.

Moving on into the latter half of the fourth century, we find Athanasius (c. 296-373) — the famous bishop of the African city of Alexandria and a courageous opponent of heresies — writing in a letter: "We know bishops who still work [miraculous] signs." Far away in what is now France, Hilary (c. 315-367), bishop of Poitiers, also spoke of the gifts currently functioning in the church, specifying tongues, prophecy, healing, miracles and others from Paul's list in 1 Corinthians 12.

Hilary's younger contemporary in the same region, Martin (d. 397), bishop of Tours, was busy working miracles similar to those attributed to the apostles in the book of Acts. Tearing down pagan altars and preaching to the barbarians, his evangelistic message was confirmed by signs and wonders that convinced his listeners he was proclaiming the truth. Martin manifested prophecy, healings, exorcisms, raising of the dead and other miracles.

Meanwhile, in the eastern Mediterranean, bishop Epiphanius of Salamis (c. 315-403) was still arguing with the Montanists in the mid-370s when he wrote: "The gift [of prophecy] is not inoperative in the Church. Quite the opposite.... The holy Church of God welcomes the same [gifts] as the Montanists, but ours are real gifts, authenticated for the Church by the Holy Spirit." In fact, this same bishop was reputed to be a prophet himself; his acquaintances reported that he ministered in personal prophecy and the words of knowledge and wisdom.

Further east still, Cyril (c. 315-387), bishop of Jerusalem, gave instructions to new Christians to expect to receive in baptism the same miraculous gifts given to the first apostles. "If you believe," he wrote, "you will receive not just remission of sins, but also do things which pass man's power. And may you be worthy of the gift of prophecy also!...Prepare yourselves for the reception of the heavenly gifts."

Crossing into the fifth century, we can note again Augustine's carefully documented records of the miracles in his diocese, including a boy raised from the dead as well as healings of paralysis, breast cancer, hernias, blindness and demon possession. We also have in Augustine's account a fascinating description of two people being healed after they experienced what modern charismatics would call being "slain in the Spirit."

As Augustine's records show, bishops were by no means the only Christians to witness or even to work miracles. That reality is confirmed by the *Sayings of the Fathers*, an anonymous collection of anecdotes and proverbs from the fourth and fifth centuries. This fascinating work tells about a number of Christians in the deserts of the Near East who practiced personal prophecy, words of knowledge and wisdom, exorcism, healings and other miracles.

Typical of these anecdotes is the story told about Joseph of Panephysis, who once received out-of-town visitors seeking his wise advice on a question about fasting. Before they could even ask the question, he answered it by acting out a brief parable and explaining the meaning. "When they heard it," the report says, "they were astonished that he knew what they intended to ask him, and they glorified God."

The Middle Ages

In the early Middle Ages, reports of miraculous giftings continued throughout the church. Severus (c. 465-538), patriarch of Antioch in Syria, wrote about sixth-century incidents of healings, words of wisdom and knowledge, prophecy and miracles. On the other end of the Mediterranean, Benedict (c. 480-550) shook Italy with his gifts of healing, prophecy and miracles. Two Gregories of that century — Pope Gregory the Great (c. 540-604) and Gregory, bishop of Tours (c. 540-594) — chronicled the miracles and giftings of a number of Christian leaders like these who lived throughout Europe. The latter Gregory reasoned that his account was important because if healings didn't happen in his own time, who would believe that they had ever happened or would ever happen again?

The seventh century saw an eruption of miraculous signs in Britain, where Aidan (d. 651), bishop of Lindisfarne, and his successor, Cuthbert (d. 687), demonstrated signs and wonders in their missionary work. These men manifested miracles, prophetic gifts and healings of the blind, lame and injured, as well as resurrections of the dead.

Cuthbert, who as a child received a personal prophecy from a three-year-old playmate that he would one day be a "priest and prelate," was himself miraculously healed twice. As an adult he frequently predicted events in the life of those around him and healed those suffering from serious illnesses and injuries, so that crowds seeking help surrounded him wherever he traveled.

In the eighth through eleventh centuries we continue to hear about gifts and miracles from the furthest borders of the Christian world. Joseph Hazzaya (born c. 710) of Syria wrote beautifully of the signs of the Holy Spirit working within the believer, apparently based on his own experience, as well as that of others. He spoke of both supernatural knowledge and tongues, which he called "a flow of spiritual speech" accompanied by jubilation and praise. Back in Europe, Ulrich of Augsburg (c. 890-973) worked miracles throughout Germany;

Anselm (1033-1109), theologian and bishop of Canterbury, performed healings and other miracles across England and ministered prophetically.

On into the twelfth century, chroniclers such as William of Malmesbury (1080-1109) and Orderic Vitalis (exact dates unknown) were collecting accounts of miracles, especially healings, of their time. Many of the accounts of individual miracles were written down as they were reported to officials, who kept the records with special care. Famous for their miracles, healings, prophecy and words of knowledge and wisdom in this century were men like Hugh of Lincoln (1140-1200) in England and Bernard of Clairveaux (1090-1153) in France.

The life of Francis of Assisi (1182-1226), one of the most famous of medieval miracle-workers, takes us into the thirteenth century. We should note that during this same century, Thomas Aquinas (1225-1274) — unquestionably the greatest theologian of the Middle Ages — was not busy hammering out arguments about why miracles no longer took place. Instead, in his *Summa Theologica*, a masterpiece that shaped Western theology for centuries, he discussed the dynamics of how God works miracles through believers. He also recognized the continuing validity and usefulness of the gift of prophecy in the church.

Perhaps the most famous of the supernaturally gifted Christians of the fourteenth century was Catherine of Siena (1347-1380), whose profound insights into the Christian life made her one of only two women in history to be designated a "doctor of the church." Catherine worked miracles, including resurrections, and was known to demonstrate personal prophecy and words of knowledge and wisdom in conversations frequently with those who sought her counsel.

Catherine's gifts were so widely respected that she counseled kings and even popes. In fact, she once sent a letter rebuking a pope for failing to keep a secret vow he had made to the Lord years before. He had never disclosed the vow to another human, but God revealed it to Catherine so she could hold him accountable.

The Modern Period

The period from the end of the Middle Ages down to the present is also well represented by Christians who displayed the gifts of the Holy Spirit. Documentation of miraculous events in this period became more extensive, even as the process of verification became more stringent. We could cite scores of names of men and women from the fifteenth century onward whose charismatic giftings were well attested. Claims of miracles worked by those in the Catholic church were especially subjected to intense scrutiny before the church would be willing to affirm that they were used supernaturally by God.

Miracles and supernatural giftings have been less common among modern Protestants. Sadly enough, the major Reformers rejected the validity of gifts after the passing of the apostles, so their followers had little expectation of encountering them. But the Holy Spirit still at times overcame theological biases and lack of faith.

We have scattered reports of healings, exorcisms, words of knowledge and wisdom, and even tongues among some groups in the seventeenth and eighteenth centuries, like the Quakers and Methodists in England and the Moravians in Eastern Europe.

George Fox (1624-1691), who founded the Quaker church, left behind a volume called the *Book of Miracles*, which documented in detail 150 of the healings under his ministry. John Wesley (1703-1791), founder of the Methodist movement, recorded in his diary scores of firsthand accounts of divine healing.

Nikolaus von Zinzendorf (1700-1760), who established the Moravian Brethren, stated explicitly that "apostolic powers" continued among his group: "We have had undeniable proofs thereof in the unequivocal discovery of things, persons and circumstances, which could not humanly have been discovered, in the healing of maladies in themselves incurable, such as cancers, consumptions, when the patients were in the agonies of death, etc., all by means of prayer, or of a single word."

In the early nineteenth century the congregation of the National Scottish Church in London began experiencing supernatural healings and the gift of tongues under the ministry of Edward Irving (1792-1834). A decade later saw the birth of a healing ministry for Johann Blumhardt, a German Lutheran pastor who in 1843 prayed for a dying young girl. Her supernatural healing at his hands and others that soon followed caused a sensation across Europe.

In 1851 a young Swiss florist, Dorothea Trudel, made headlines when she anointed with oil several of her coworkers whose illnesses had resisted all medical treatment. They were instantaneously healed by her prayer, and soon the sick were coming to her from all over the continent.

Charles Cullis (1833-1892), a medical doctor in Boston, reached a turning point in his life when in 1870 he witnessed the miraculous healing of a woman who had been completely immobilized by a brain tumor for five months. He spent the rest of his life ministering in the healing gifts and bringing the reality of miracles to the public's attention.

Cullis's ministry and writings convinced a number of the leading evangelical figures of the late nineteenth century to embrace miracles and healing as normative, including South African churchman Andrew Murray; Christian & Missionary Alliance founder A.B. Simpson; and Boston pastor A.J. Gordon, founder of Gordon College.

At the turn of the century some of the most dramatic manifestations of God's healing power occurred in the ministry of women such as Maria Woodworth-Etter (1844-1924). Newspapers across the country covered her revival meetings; some reported firsthand that hopeless cripples walked, hearing was restored to the deaf and other miraculous healings took place.

Perhaps the Christian of our century who exhibited the most amazing spiritual gifts was Padre Pio of Pietrelcina (1887-1968). This Italian demonstrated all the gifts the budding Pentecostal movement in America was focusing on: tongues and interpretation (in his case, known languages he had never studied); healings; prophecy; words of knowledge and wisdom; and miracles. The miracles of healing in particular are documented extensively in hundreds of testimonials.

Since World War II some of the more startling demonstrations of power and prophetic knowledge were presented by healing evangelist William Branham (1909-1965); hundreds testified to his remarkable gifting in healing, discerning diseases and knowing the secrets of others' hearts. In 1951 Branham's gift received worldwide attention when William Upshaw, a U.S. congressman from California who had been crippled from birth, was healed under his ministry. Sadly enough, however, Branham's later years took him into eccentric teachings and sparked a cultic following that has remained since his death.

As the postwar healing revival with its broader appeal to mainline church members gave birth to the charismatic movement, it focused new and increasing attention on spiritual gifts and miracles. American evangelist Oral Roberts and others have been widely recognized for their healing gifts in particular. Roberts, healed of tuberculosis as a youth, profoundly influenced the course of American Christianity by using television to take his healing ministry into the homes of millions.

Accounts of miracles, especially healings, continue to flow from a variety of ministries today, such as the great overseas crusades of Reinhard Bonnke and Mahesh Chavda and the more quiet work of Francis and Judith MacNutt. Verifiable revelatory gifts, such as prophecy, visions and words of knowledge and wisdom, are amply demonstrated in the ministries of men such as Paul Cain and Bill Hamon.

These are just a few of the better-known figures whose gifts are attested to by many Christians, but of course their ministries by no means constitute the whole of modern-day miracles and supernatural gifts. Since the early days of the Pentecostal movement, countless testimonies have continued to accumulate that God continues to work miraculously through His people.

Two Millennia of Evidence

Recently a well-known fundamentalist teacher, attempting to challenge charismatic claims for valid gifts today, asked: "What happened to miracles, healings, signs and wonders in the nineteen hundred years since the apostles passed from the scene? Was the Holy Spirit inactive during that time?"

This brief summary of believers who have borne witness to spiritual gifts over nineteen centuries should answer those questions conclusively. The Holy Spirit has by no means been inactive; God has been supernaturally intervening in the world's affairs through His gifted people all along. To sum up, we can turn to the words of Jaroslav Pelikan, a former professor of history and religious studies at Yale and one of the world's foremost church historians (not himself a charismatic): "The history of the church has never been altogether without the spontaneous gifts of the Holy Spirit."

No doubt the historical record doesn't fit the theology of many Christians. Sadly enough, they have tended to ignore the evidence or deny its validity because of a narrow mind-set.

Nevertheless, the testimonies to God's power remain. From the first century to the twentieth, from Antioch to Azusa Street, from Africans, Arabs, Europeans, Americans and Asians, the accounts have been gathered and preserved to challenge the skepticism of unbelievers and to build the faith of believers. In the light of such overwhelming evidence, the church today can look to the *past* with gratitude for what God has done, to the *present* with faith in His still-awesome power and to the *future* with hope for the great miracles He will yet accomplish.

Paul Thigpen received his bachelor's degree in religious studies from Yale University and a master's degree in historical theology from Emory University. He is completing work on a Ph.D. in historical theology from Emory University. His writing credits include children's books, teaching books and hundreds of magazine articles. He lives in Florida with his wife, Leisa, and their two children.

This chapter originally appeared as an article in the September 1992 issue of *Charisma & Christian Life*, with contributions from *Charisma* associate editor John Archer.

THREE

Answering Challenges to the Historical Evidence

Five common objections are refuted with logic, Scripture and facts.

BY PAUL THIGPEN

When confronted with the numerous historical accounts of miracles and spiritual gifts after the time of the first apostles, Christians whose theology doesn't allow for such events typically raise several challenges. Here are the more common ones, with a response.

1. *You can't trust the reliability of these sources; people back then were credulous and superstitious.*

This is the same challenge offered by non-Christian skeptics when confronted with the miracles in the Bible.

No doubt reliability of historical sources must rank high on our list of criteria for credibility. And no one would argue that the Middle Ages in particular abounded in rather silly supernatural tales, many of which were attached to famous Christian figures. But even after such sources are eliminated, we still have a massive amount of material from across the centuries whose weight cannot be dismissed without dismissing some of the most respected Christian leaders of history — people such as Irenaeus, Augustine, Catherine of Siena and Wesley.

In addition, we should remember that we are most often dealing, not with anonymous stories, but with carefully compiled documentary evidence, provided firsthand from people who experienced healings in their own bodies or were eyewitnesses to such events. Augustine's thorough research is only one example.

Writers such as Theodoret, who reported miracles among the desert Christians in the Middle East; Severus, who wrote the life of Martin of Tours; and Bede, who wrote the history of England, all noted soberly that they only recorded what they could be sure about, gleaned from reliable sources and, when possible, from eyewitnesses. Wrote Severus: "I have written nothing of which I have not certain knowledge and evidence. I should, in fact, have preferred to be silent rather than to narrate things which are false."

In fact, beginning in the tenth century, church officials developed a rather rigorous process of investigation for verifying miracles. Written accounts had to be submitted with details of the circumstances surrounding an event that was claimed to be miraculous. For healings, the name of the person concerned, where he or she lived, the illness, the names of witnesses, when and how the person came to the one who manifested the miracle and how the cure was effected were required as proof. Witnesses were summoned to Rome to state the facts in question, or assessors were sent to examine the witnesses and report on their reliability.

In light of these circumstances, mistrust of historical material collected in this way simply reveals a bias against the supernatural. Just as many non-Christians immediately conclude that a biblical passage is merely legend when it records a miracle — no matter how credible the source otherwise — some Christians take a closed approach to church history. They agree that, because they already know miracles didn't happen, any account of one must be dismissed as a fabrication.

2. *Most of the people who made these claims were in fanatical fringe groups.*

This particular claim is usually buttressed by references to the ancient Montanist heretics who focused on prophetic gifts; self-proclaimed "prophets" from the Middle Ages who wandered the highways of Europe preaching political revolution; and more recent heretical groups such as the Shakers or Mormons, who also claimed to speak in tongues.

Though such fringe groups gave spiritual gifts a bad reputation by claiming them for themselves, the list of writers affirming the continuation of these gifts in the orthodox Christian community is overwhelming. Irenaeus, Augustine, Gregory, Aquinas and many others from among the central leadership of the church in their day could hardly be called fanatics, sectarians or heretics. In fact, in the Montanist controversy, the continual refrain of mainline church leaders was not that prophecy had ceased, but that Montanist prophecy was false and prophecy in the true church was genuine. The historian Eusebius quoted one anti-Montanist writer as insisting (probably based on Ephesians 2:20): "The apostle [Paul] declares that the prophetic gifts should continue to be in the entire church until the second coming."

As church historian Jaroslav Pelikan has noted, the charismatic gifts have appeared throughout church history — even in the most orthodox of groups "where the authority of the apostolic norms has been incontestable."

3. *The miraculous phenomena recorded in church history are essentially different from those in the Bible.*

This objection usually takes one of three forms.

• The New Testament miracles and spiritual gifts were worked through human agencies (the apostles), but later miracles are not. God may on a rare occasion cause a miracle to happen today, according to this position, but supernatural giftings are no longer given to Christians.

Just a brief glance at the historical records in chapter 2 should dispel this claim. Again and again the records deal, not with a miracle granted in response to the prayers of the church, but with individual believers who were gifted supernaturally to work miracles repeatedly.

• Miracles claimed for later generations were not as spectacular as those in the New Testament.

This conclusion depends on what is meant by "spectacular." All the types of miracles worked by Jesus and the apostles recorded in the New Testament have been reproduced in later years by their successors, just as Jesus had promised (John 14:12). What could be considered the most spectacular miracle of all — raising the dead — has been reported more than four hundred times throughout church history.

• Unless a person who is claimed to be supernaturally gifted can exercise that gift at will, the gift isn't valid.

If this were true, Jesus' gift wouldn't have been valid. The Scripture tells us that at times He couldn't work great miracles because of the people's unbelief (Matt. 13:58). It also notes that at some times "the power of the Lord was present...to heal" (Luke 5:17, NIV), implying that there were times when the power was *not* present. Nor could the apostle Paul always heal those who were sick (see 2 Tim. 4:2).

The reality is that many of the Christians who have had extraordinary spiritual gifts throughout history displayed a long-term pattern of miracles. But they, like Jesus and Paul, were not always able to exercise them, for whatever reasons.

4. *Even if these miracles throughout church history were verifiable, their validity must be questioned because their scarcity in later times doesn't parallel their frequency in the New Testament church.*

No doubt the frequency of miracles in later generations cannot compare to that in the New Testament accounts. That sad reality was noted from early times even by those who affirmed that the gifts were still in operation. When they asked why the gap existed, however, most came to the same conclusion: The later church lacks the power of the first Christians because it also lacks their purity and faith. Most of the recorded instances of supernatural gifting since then have involved individual believers who were also known for their extraordinary personal holiness.

This isn't to say we must earn the gifts by our works. Nor is it to say God can't choose to work supernaturally through less-than-holy people: After all, Samson was no model of virtue (Judg. 13-16), and the high priest Caiaphas prophesied the word of the Lord even as He was plotting Jesus' death (John 11:45-53). But it does suggest that, just as Jesus' own miracles were limited by the unbelief of some people, our own spiritual immaturity may limit our exercise of the gifts.

In addition, we should note that the frequency of New Testament miracles has at times been overstated. Contrary to one fundamentalist writer's claims, the Bible does not show that when Jesus walked the earth, "disease was, in effect, banished from Palestine." After the resurrection there were still sick people around who sought the apostles for help. As the same writer notes, the book of Acts itself doesn't record any miracles in Jerusalem after the martyrdom of Stephen.

5. *Because many recorded miracles have been worked by people whose theology is questionable, these miracles must be dismissed, for God would not work signs and wonders to confirm wrong doctrine.*

The problem with this position is twofold: First, those who take it often have defined rather narrowly what is correct theology, assuming that people who don't agree with them even on minor issues are heretical. If we ruled out everyone who isn't fundamentalist from the potential ranks of the spiritually gifted, we would no doubt have few miracles to talk about — especially considering that the fundamentalist position typically prevents people from exercising faith that a miracle could happen.

Second, this claim that God won't confirm wrong teaching with miracles rests on the assumption that miracles were given only for the purpose of confirming His Word. This was certainly one of the reasons for the miracles worked by Jesus and the apostles (Mark 16:20; John 14:11; Acts 14:3). But miracles are also signs of God's kingdom breaking in on the world (Matt. 12:28), a taste of "the powers of the coming age" (Heb. 6:4-5).

In addition, the Lord showed His power in this way because He had compassion on His people and wanted to meet their physical needs (Matt. 14:14-21). He worked miracles to heal people who hurt, feed people who were hungry and deliver people in cruel bondage to the devil.

This means that God may very well display supernatural power through human instruments whose theology is lacking — not because He wants to confirm their teaching, but simply because He wants to give the world a foretaste of the kingdom and minister to His people. If necessary, He'll work through imperfect human vessels to accomplish these purposes.

Like the man whose sight Jesus restored (John 9:25), people whose lives have been transformed by miracles, both in our day and in earlier generations, may not always know whether a particular miracle-worker's teaching is acceptable to certain religious groups. All they know is that through that person's hands, they have personally experienced the supernatural power of heaven.

For them, that's more than sufficient historical

evidence to believe that God is still working miracles through the spiritual gifts He has given His church.

Paul Thigpen received his bachelor's degree in religious studies from Yale University and a master's degree in historical theology from Emory University. He is completing work on a Ph.D. in historical theology from Emory University. His writing credits include children's books, teaching books and hundreds of magazine articles. He lives in Florida with his wife, Leisa, and their two children.

This chapter originally appeared as an article in the September 1992 issue of *Charisma & Christian Life*.

FOUR

WHY DOES GOD DO MIRACLES?

God's many purposes in performing miracles testify that the Spirit's supernatural gifts should continue in the life of the church.

BY JACK DEERE

During most of my academic career, I was confident that I could prove that the miraculous gifts of the Holy Spirit had ceased at the end of the first century A.D. As a professor at a well-respected dispensationalist seminary, I thought I had the biblical, theological and historical arguments to demonstrate that such gifts as miracles, healings, prophecies and tongues were limited to New Testament times. But my confidence in my ability, or anyone else's ability, to prove this assertion was fundamentally shaken.

It wasn't shaken by having seen or experienced any sort of miraculous phenomena, though in the years since then I have seen a number of miraculous works of the Spirit. Rather my perspective changed as I re-examined the biblical data used to prove the disappearance of the miraculous gifts. As I gained a better understanding from the Bible of the purposes for miracles, I came to believe that supernatural gifts have a legitimate function in the church today.

If the only purpose of miracles was to authenticate the apostles — as I once thought — then one *might* be able to make a strong biblical case that miraculous ministry died out with the apostles. But other scriptural purposes can be shown for miracles — purposes rooted in God's character and works. And God's ongoing purposes in performing miracles testify that the Spirit's supernatural gifts should continue in the life of the church.

Cessationism

In the early twentieth century the most influential proponent of cessationism — the theory that miraculous spiritual gifts ceased with the deaths of the apostles — was Princeton theologian Benjamin B. Warfield. In his 1918 book *Counterfeit Miracles*, Warfield argued that miracles were intended solely to authenticate the apostles: "These...were part of the credentials of the apostles as the authoritative agents of God in founding the church. Their function thus confined them to distinctively the apostolic church, and they *necessarily passed away* with it" (italics added).

But if miracles belonged exclusively to the apostles, as Warfield contends, why would anyone outside the apostolic office do them? That the sphere of miraculous ministry extended beyond the apostles is seen in a number of New Testament examples, such as:

- deacons Stephen (Acts 6:8) and Philip (8:6)
- Ananias (9:10-18)
- Barnabas (14:3)
- among believers in Corinth (1 Cor. 12:8-10) and Galatia (Gal. 3:5)

In quoting Joel's prophecy on the day of Pentecost, Peter lists supernatural gifts such as prophecy, dreams and visions as manifestations of the Spirit's outpouring available to all. The gift of prophecy, in particular, is mentioned numerous times as operating in individuals not identified as apostles. Some examples include:

- Agabus (Acts 11:28; 21:10)
- the prophets at Antioch (Acts 13:1)
- Judas and Silas (Acts 15:32)
- Philip's daughters (Acts 21:9)
- among believers in Rome (Rom. 12:6) and Thessalonica (1 Thess. 5:20)

Moreover, after Pentecost the whole Christian community prayed that God would grant them boldness to witness by healing and doing "signs and wonders" through the name of Jesus (Acts 4:23-31). In this prayer for power to proclaim the gospel, there was no suggestion that such miracles were to be performed solely by the apostles.

This churchwide prayer would seem, then, to be in accord with Christ's declaration in Mark 16:17-18: "These signs will follow those who believe: In My name they will cast out demons...they will lay hands on the sick, and they will recover." (Despite questions concerning the authorship of this passage by some New Testament scholars, few would question that it reflects what the early church believed and experienced.)

Rather than showing that miracles were performed solely by the apostles, the Scriptures suggest that miraculous gifts were common among New Testament believers. Because miracles were not confined to the apostolic office, there's no reason to believe the death of the apostles would have caused these gifts to disappear from the church.

Jesus and His Message

The New Testament indicates that a primary function of miracles is to authenticate the Person and work of Jesus. In the Gospels Jesus' mighty works confirmed a number of claims, such as:

- The Father sent Jesus (John 5:6).
- The Father is in Jesus, and Jesus is in the Father (John 10:37-38).
- The words of Jesus are from the Father (John 14:10-11).
- Jesus has authority to forgive sins (Mark 2:10-11).
- In Jesus the kingdom of God has come (Matt. 12:28).
- Jesus is the Messiah (Matt. 11:1-6).
- Jesus is the Son of God (Matt. 14:25-33).

Likewise, the miracles of the apostles bore witness to Jesus and His message as genuinely from God. Mark 16:20, for example, says the disciples "preached everywhere, the Lord working with them and confirming the word through the accompanying signs." Scripture says signs and wonders bear "witness to the word of His grace" (Acts 14:3; see also Heb. 2:3-4).

An Authentic Message

If Jesus and the message about Jesus required miraculous confirmation in the first century, why isn't such authentication required today?

Some cessationists answer that the miracles of Jesus, culminating in His resurrection from the dead, proved once for all His deity and the reality of His mission. But if this were so, why is the message about Jesus authenticated with the miracles in the book of Acts? After Jesus' resurrection, God was still confirming the gospel with miracles.

Other cessationists answer that, since this confirmation is now enshrined in the Bible, the Bible itself replaces the need for the miraculous in its authenticating function. This assertion, of course, is made without direct New Testament evidence. Nowhere in the Bible are we told that the written Word of God replaces the need for miraculous confirmation of the divine message.

Still others answer that first-century Christianity required the confirmation of miracles because its central message — the death and resurrection of an obscure Jewish carpenter — would scarcely have been believed otherwise. Once Christianity became established as a legitimate choice among the world's religions, they say, it no longer required miracles to prove the genuineness of the gospel.

Not only does this explanation lack any scriptural support, but it also demeans the power inherent in the message about Jesus. More than that, it substitutes world opinion for the miraculous power of God, hardly a trade that anyone would want to make today or that could be justified theologically.

Did the need to confirm the divine nature of the gospel end in the first century?

I don't believe so. No scriptural text indicates that God has done away with the authenticating function of the miraculous. Nor is there any evidence that the church no longer needs miraculous confirmation for the message about the Lord Jesus Christ.

Nevertheless, it's not uncommon for orthodox theologians to demean the authenticating function of the miraculous. In his "Distinguishing Marks of a Work of the Spirit of God," eighteenth-century preacher Jonathan Edwards wrote: "I do not expect a restoration of these miraculous gifts in the approaching glorious times of the church, nor do I desire it.... It does not appear to me that there is any need of those extraordinary gifts.... I have seen so much of the power of God in a more excellent way as to convince me that God can easily do it without."

This is not a view that Jesus or the New Testament shares.

Jesus said, "I have a *greater witness* than John's; for the works which the Father has given Me to finish — the very works that I do — bear witness of Me, that the Father has sent Me" (John 5:36, italics added). In contrast to the testimony of John the Baptist, who did no miracles (John 10:41), Jesus' testimony was confirmed by His mighty works. This miraculous confirmation, according to Jesus, makes His testimony greater than that of John's. Thus Jesus acknowledged that a message confirmed by miraculous works has greater proof of its authenticity than one without such confirmation.

The Glory of God

Beyond confirming the gospel message, miracles also bring glory to the Father and to the Son. This is the dominant purpose in the raising of Lazarus. Jesus told the disciples, "This sickness is not unto death, but for the *glory of God*, that the Son of God may be glorified through it" (John 11:4, italics added). Later He told Martha, "Did I not say to you that if you would believe you would see the *glory of God?*" (John 11:40, italics added).

Peter explained the healing of the lame man at the temple gate in this way: "Why look so intently at us, as though by our own power or godliness we had made this man walk? The God of Abraham, Isaac, and Jacob, the God of our fathers, *glorified His Servant Jesus*" (Acts 3:12-13, italics added).

It was normal for people to observe the mighty works of Jesus and respond by glorifying God. In Matthew 15:30-31, the multitudes "glorified the God of Israel" after seeing the lame, blind and mute healed (see also Luke 5:24-26; 7:16).

And Jesus expected people who were recipients of the miraculous power of God to do this. After only one of the ten lepers He healed returned to give thanks, Jesus said, "Were there not ten cleansed? But where are the nine? Were there not any found who returned to *give glory to God* except this foreigner" (Luke 17:17-18, italics added).

The miracles of Jesus also *revealed* God's glory, disclosing His power and majesty. When Jesus turned water into wine, John says this "manifested His glory" (John 2:11).

God's Compassion and Mercy

Another divine motivation for the working of miracles stems from the compassion and mercy of God. The healing ministry of Jesus was motivated by His love for those suffering: "And when Jesus went out He saw a great multitude; and He was moved with compassion for them, and healed their sick" (Matt. 14:14).

His compassion motivated Him to heal lepers (Mark 1:41-42), the demonized (Mark 9:22) and the blind (Matt. 20:34) and even to raise the dead (Luke 7:12-15). In the Gospel of Matthew, the feeding of the four thousand is motivated not by Jesus' desire to demonstrate His messianic claims, but by His compassion on the multitude (Matt. 15:32).

Likewise, Jesus heals the blind (Matt. 9:27-31), the demonized (Matt. 15:27-23) and the lepers (Luke 17:13-14) in response to their cries for mercy. The healing of the most severely demon-possessed person in the New Testament is attributed ultimately to the mercy of God (Mark 5:19).

Salvation

Another purpose for miracles is their role in stimulating and inviting faith. The New Testament gives a number of examples of people who repented and believed through the miracles of Jesus and the apostles: Peter (Luke 5:8-11), the man born blind (John 9) and the proconsul Sergius Paulus (Acts 13:11-12), to name a few.

Jesus Himself believed His miracles alone should have been enough to bring whole cities, such as Bethsaida and Capernaum, to salvation, though they did not repent (Matt. 11:20-24).

John's Gospel makes it clear that Jesus' miracles were done and recorded to lead people to faith: "Jesus did many other signs in the presence of His disciples, which are not written in this book; but these are written that you may believe that Jesus is the Christ, the Son of God, and that believing you may have life in His name" (John 20:30-31).

Miracles also serve to open doors for evangelism. This is seen in the story of the man Jesus delivered from a legion of demons: "Go home to your friends," Jesus told him, "and tell them what great things the Lord has done for you, and how He has had compassion on you. And he departed and began to proclaim in Decapolis all that Jesus had done for him; and all marveled" (Mark 5:19-20). A similar incident occurred with the Samaritan woman after her encounter with Jesus (John 4:28-42).

The power of miracles to further the preaching of the gospel is an important theme in the book of Acts:

- At Pentecost the miraculous descent of the Holy Spirit and the resultant speaking in tongues drew the large crowds so that Peter might proclaim the gospel to them (Acts 2).
- When the people saw the lame man who was healed by Peter walking and praising God, they ran to Solomon's porch, where Peter was able to preach to them (Acts 3:1-26).
- The apostolic miracles have a similar effect in Acts 5:12-16. That the high priest accused the apostles of filling Jerusalem with their doctrine (Acts 5:28) is evidence of the power of the miraculous to open doors for evangelism.
- The city of Samaria listened to Philip because

of the miracles they saw him perform (Acts 8:6-8).

- When the paralytic Aeneas was healed, Luke notes that "all who dwelt at Lydda and Sharon saw him and turned to the Lord" (Acts 9:35).
- The raising of Dorcas "became known throughout all Joppa, and many believed on the Lord" (Acts 9:42).
- Many Ephesians believed because of the apostle Paul's miraculous ministry (Acts 19:11-20).

Sovereign Purposes

Some New Testament miracles seem to be simply sovereign works of the Lord without a clear explanation. At the pool of Bethesda, for example, Jesus healed only one paralytic, though a great multitude of sick people lay around the pool that day (John 5:1-15).

The answer to why Jesus healed only that particular person is given a few verses later: "The Son can do nothing of Himself, but what He sees the Father do; for whatever He does, the Son also does in like manner" (John 5:19).

This verse gives one of the cardinal principles of Jesus' ministry: The initiative for the miraculous in Jesus' ministry did not begin with Him but with His Father. He healed only the people He saw His Father healing. The only firm reason for the healing of the paralytic that we can derive from the context of John 5 is that the Father willed it, and Jesus executed His Father's will.

A similar explanation might be offered for the miraculous deliverance of Peter from prison in Acts 12. Why did the Lord allow James to be martyred, yet send an angel to deliver Peter from death? One might argue that it was because the church prayed for Peter, but without a doubt the church prayed for James also.

We are ultimately faced with the conclusion that sometimes the Lord works miracles for His own sovereign purposes without giving any explanation for His actions to His followers.

The Kingdom of God

Most New Testament scholars agree that Jesus' central message concerned the good news of the kingdom of God: "Jesus went about all Galilee...preaching the gospel of the kingdom, and healing all kinds of sickness" (Matt. 4:23). This message of God's kingly rule also marked the preaching of the early church (Acts 8:12; 20:25).

The New Testament pictures Satan as the enemy of the kingdom of God and the source of all manner of physical suffering (Acts 10:38). Thus, the miracles of healing and deliverance that accompanied the proclamation of the kingdom manifested the present reality of God's rule and His victory over Satan's domain:

- "If I cast out demons by the Spirit of God," Jesus said, "surely the kingdom of God has come upon you" (Matt. 12:28).
- As an extension of His own ministry, Jesus gave the twelve apostles "power and authority over all demons, and to cure diseases. He sent them to preach the kingdom of God and to heal the sick" (Luke 9:1-2).
- Jesus sent out the seventy disciples and instructed them to "heal the sick...and say to them, 'The kingdom of God has come near to you' " (Luke 10:9).

Demons, disease and death — which all entered creation at humanity's fall — will be completely banished in the age to come. Until then the miraculous power that delivers people from bondage to Satan demonstrates that the kingdom of God has broken in upon this present evil age.

The close connection between miracles and the kingdom finds precise theological formulation in Paul's statement that "the kingdom of God is not in word but in power" (1 Cor. 4:20). Miraculous power is more than temporary evidence of God's kingdom; it's a characteristic of His kingdom.

Why Miracles?

Miracles bring glory to God and to His Son, flow out of His compassion and mercy, open doors for evangelism and lead people to faith in Christ.

Miracles are a perpetual demonstration of Christ's power as living and glorified, and a visible token of His kingdom, which is both present and soon-coming.

Miracles are not something the church of Jesus Christ can do without. Done in continuation of all that He did and taught, these mighty works accomplish God's purposes and reveal the power and nature of our Savior and King.

Jack Deere, Th.D., a former professor at Dallas Theological Seminary, is writing a book on the biblical basis for ministry in the supernatural.

This chapter originally appeared as an article in the September 1992 issue of *Charisma & Christian Life*, with contributions from *Charisma* associate editor John Archer.

FIVE

Why Miracles Are for Today

Oral Roberts's personal encounter with miracles can help you believe.

BY ORAL ROBERTS

Some claim that all reports of miracles are false. They have already concluded that miracles *don't* happen because they *can't* happen. God doesn't do those things anymore, they would say. There is little difference between this logic and the logic of a skeptical theologian who is certain that the miracle accounts in the Bible are all myths and legends. He does not believe the biblical accounts because he has already concluded that miracles can *never* happen.

Why are miracles for today? A miracle settles the issue. Jesus said that signs were to confirm the word that was preached by the apostles (Mark 16:17). When Dorcas was healed by a miracle performed through Peter, the preaching of the apostles was confirmed, and the whole town believed that Jesus was the Messiah.

We don't need miracles today because we have the written Word, say those who doubt modern-day miracles. Are you sure? There are more people alive today than ever before who need to see confirmation of the truth of God's Word. For them the issue is not settled.

One day a man walked up to me and said, "Oral Roberts, every time I hear you preach, you're talking about miracles. Well, I just want to tell you that I don't believe in miracles."

Quick as a flash, the Lord gave me a word for him. "You will when you need one!"

I'll never forget the look that came on his face. "I hadn't thought of that," he replied.

"Mister," I said, "I was desperately ill with a terminal disease at a time when there was no medical help for me. Although I had no chance to live, my family held out to me the hope of a miracle from God. When they told me miracles are for today, I grabbed hold of that with what little faith I had, and I got my miracle!"

"You sure don't look to me like you've ever been real sick," he said.

"That is because the Lord settled the issue."

I had run away from home at sixteen to escape my parents' religion and poverty. A judge in Ada, Oklahoma, allowed me to live in his house and use his books to study law. My dream as a high school student was to become governor of Oklahoma.

I was playing in a basketball tournament that year when suddenly everything began to blur before my eyes. I stumbled and collapsed on the floor.

Blood came from my mouth.

My coach rushed over and, with the help of others, put me in the back seat of his car. “Oral,” he said, “you’re going home.”

My parents put me in bed and called for a doctor. Although many Pentecostals of that day clung to divine healing and had little to do with medical doctors, my father was not that way. One day my father came into my bedroom after the doctor had left. Tears welled up in his eyes.

“Papa,” I asked, “what’s wrong?”

“Oral, you have tuberculosis in both lungs.”

This was 1934. There was no penicillin, no miracle drug. Death was staring me in the face.

Then one day something happened that changed my life. My sister, Jewell, felt led to come seventeen miles to our house to share a message from God. She came to my bedside and said, “Oral, God is going to heal you.”

It was as though a light was turned on in my soul. All at once I awakened and became aware of Jesus. With those few words my sister let me know Jesus was interested in my life. He knew me and cared about me.

Shortly after this my brother Elmer came to our house. He had been to a tent revival where an evangelist was praying for the sick. Elmer came into my bedroom and said, “Oral, get up. God is going to heal you.”

As I rode on a mattress in the back of Elmer’s little car, I knew God was going to heal me. God spoke to my heart and promised to heal me. He also called me to carry His healing power to my generation. Though I didn’t have any idea what that meant, I knew my life was in His hands. I have never ceased to believe that.

At the tent revival the evangelist put his hands on my head and prayed, "Thou foul disease! I command you in the name of Jesus Christ to come out of this boy's lungs. Loose him, and let him go!"

The next thing I knew I was running back and forth across the platform shouting, "I am healed! I am healed!"

My parents took me back to my doctor for another examination. My lungs were fluoroscoped and found perfectly healthy!

"Son," the doctor exclaimed, "just forget you ever had TB! Your lungs are as sound as a dollar."

God had settled the matter for me.

I've been sent to spread the gospel of Bible deliverance to people in virtually all walks of life, sick or well, poor or rich. And I can honestly say I have seen or sensed in every one a deep consciousness that not only are miracles for us today, but we don't have a prayer without miracles making the difference in our lives and our generation.

The common thread running through the soul of human beings is the inborn understanding that miracles are real. Regardless of whether they can explain it or pay sufficient attention to the way God created them, I'm absolutely convinced everybody knows something about miracles, and they cannot escape it in their consciousness. If nothing else, they are curious to see a miracle. And when an undeniable miracle happens before their very eyes, they are visibly affected by it.

I remember, for example, one of my crusades in the Far East. It was one of the most difficult in all my healing ministry.

First, the people were very superstitious.

Second, my interpreters had a hard time putting my sermons from the Bible in terms the crowds could relate to, and I was frustrated by it.

Third, it was a highly armed country. Each night hundreds of soldiers lined the walls with a watchful eye on what this American preacher was doing with his preaching and the miracles of his God.

Worst of all, the sick people before me in the healing line did not want me to touch them when I prayed for their healing. People raised in the Chinese culture typically don't like to be touched.

There were few apparent results, so I was discouraged and baffled. An American missionary called me aside. "Brother Roberts," he said, "let me explain the situation to you," and he told me about their fear of being touched as I laid hands on them in my prayers.

"What am I going to do?" I asked.

"We the sponsoring pastors have called a special time of prayer and fasting before tomorrow night's service for God to give the breakthrough. It'll take a miracle this country has never seen."

The following evening the auditorium was jammed and suffocatingly hot. Hostility rose like an evil cloud. Nothing was going right. I couldn't feel the anointing I always felt. The sick came, and I prayed; they walked off or were carried off. It was a critical moment.

Then a young Chinese mother stood before me with a large goiter on her neck that the audience could plainly see. I knew God had used me to heal goiters, but this was a different scene. I remember saying to myself, Well, I'm failing; the crusade is failing; what have I got to lose? I'll command this goiter to go, in Jesus' name. It'll take a miracle of miracles for anything to change things here.

I forgot where I was. That goiter stood out before me like a rattlesnake ready to strike at me. I felt the devil close by. Just then the presence of God came into my right hand, and my spirit came alive in the Holy Spirit. Suddenly my hand was on that goiter, and my voice rang out like a thunderclap.

"You foul goiter, I command you in the name of Jesus Christ of Nazareth — you come off this woman's neck. Loose her, and let her go free!"

The goiter vanished! The woman's hands flew to her neck, and she screamed. I heard feet shuffling. The soldiers stampeded onto the stage. Their leader seized the woman, rubbed his hand on her neck and asked her in loud Chinese where the goiter had gone.

As she tried to explain, I had the interpreter tell me what she was saying. "A miracle!" she said. "God took my goiter away. This man (pointing at me) prayed; I believed. Goiter is gone!"

In seconds the entire atmosphere changed. Soldiers fell at my feet, crying, calling on God. In probably no more than ten minutes a thousand or more had accepted Christ as their personal Savior.

On that night of miracles God first said to me, "A miracle settles the issue!" This is your hour for your miracle. Turn your faith loose and seize it!

Oral Roberts is in his fifth decade of leading evangelistic and healing crusades. He is the president and founder of Oral Roberts University in Tulsa, Oklahoma, and has sent medical missionaries—combining medicine and prayer—throughout the world. Roberts lives in Tulsa with his wife, Evelyn.

This chapter originally appeared as an article in the November 1991 issue of *Charisma & Christian Life*.

CHRISTIAN LIFE BOOKS
Tools for Spirit-led Living

If you enjoyed *Miracles Never Cease!*, we would like to recommend the following books:

Effective Prayer
by John Dawson, B. J. Willhite, Francis MacNutt, Judson Cornwall and Larry Lea
Key concepts to refresh and renew your prayer life

Parents and Teachers: Equipping the Younger Saints
by David Walters
Fresh ideas for training children and youth to be soldiers for Christ

The Gifts of the Spirit
by Jack Hayford, John Wimber, Reinhard Bonnke, Judith MacNutt, Michael P. Williams, Mark A. Pearson, John Archer and Mahesh Chavda
In-depth teaching on receiving and understanding spiritual gifts

Prophecy in the Church
by Martin Scott
Practical guidelines for the use of prophecy in the church

God's Remedy for Rejection
by Derek Prince
Scriptural steps for overcoming the spiritual wound of rejection